This book belongs to

....

I am..........years old

I am..........tall

How Big is Big?
How Far is Far?
All Around Me

Illustrated by Jun Cen

LITTLE
GESTALTEN

Look up, look down, look all around. See here something small. Over there, something tall. Up in the air is the teeniest of things. Growing high out of the ground, one of the oldest of things.

But how big is huge? How teeny is tiny? How fast is slow, or how much is many?

Come take a look and discover that our planet is full of surprises ...

Smile like a Cow

How high can you count? Try counting your teeth. How many are there?

When your teeth are fully grown like an adult, you will have 32. Your mouth is a very small space for so many! Did you know that humans have the same number of teeth as a cow?

But ...

The giant armadillo has over 80 teeth, and the great white shark can have 300, which are tiny and arranged in lots of rows.

32 teeth

Human and cow

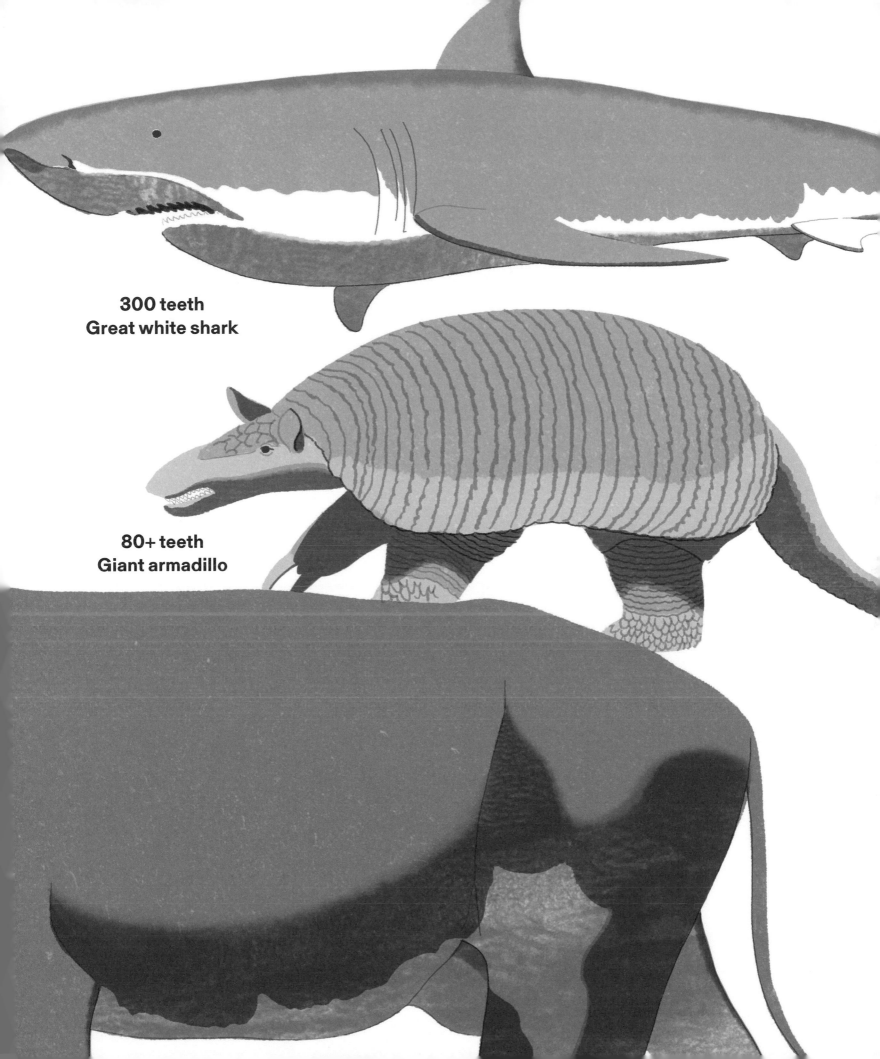

300 teeth
Great white shark

80+ teeth
Giant armadillo

Older Than the Pyramids

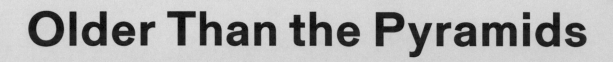

Imagine what it must be like to be older than the pyramids. Think of all the things you would have seen …

Growing quietly for thousands of years, hidden in the White Mountains in America, is the oldest living tree. The long-living pine tree is from a very old family.

There are 17 varieties that are over 4,000 years old, and the oldest is over 5,000 years old. Much, much older than the oldest pyramids from Ancient Egypt. How old are you?

Over 5,000 years ago
Oldest tree began to grow

Over 4,700 years ago
Pyramids were built

Over 2,000 years ago
Calendar years began

Your
birthday

You
today

Stretch Wide

Put your arms out very wide. Stretch, stretch, stretch! How far can you stretch them?

Did you know the length you are now stretching is the same as your height? That is not the case for other creatures.

When the wandering albatross stretches out its wings, they can stretch as wide as 11.5 feet. That's almost 2.5 times their average height!

An adult

You

A wandering albatross
11.5 feet

I Spy with My Little Eye

Your tiny little eye sees the world. But how big is that eye? The size of a ping-pong ball, or maybe a marble?

The colossal squid that swims far down in the deep ocean has eyes that are bigger than a basketball.

It is very, very dark so far down in the ocean. The colossal squid's big eyes help collect more light ... all the better to find its food.

Ping-pong ball

A human eyeball is about 0.8 – 1.0 inches across.

A colossal squid's eye is 11 inches across.

Basketball

Packed Tight!

Take a look at your parent's thumbnail. If there were hairs growing out of that nail, how many do you think could fit there? Would there be 3, or 100? Maybe 200?

In a space about that size, the fuzzy brown otter has around 100,000 hairs. It has the densest fur in the whole animal kingdom!

100,000 hairs can be as many as you have on your entire head.

Size of a thumbnail

Put your thumb here!

Flap like a Honeybee

How fast can you flap your arms in one minute?

How about one second?

A honeybee can flap its wings 230 times in just one second. Not fast enough?

Meet the tiny mosquito. It beats its wings furiously around the room. Much, much faster than you or the honeybee.

**230 times per second
Honeybee**

**800 wingbeats per second
Mosquito**

**70 times per second
Hummingbird**

You? Try it for yourself.
How many times can you
flap in a second?

Grow Fast

Overnight, you will see it grow. You can hear it creak as it stretches up to the sky. Have you ever seen something grow before? Come take a look ...

Some bamboo can grow nearly one metre in a single day. If you sit very still and watch, you might see it move upward.

How tall will you grow today, tomorrow, or even next year?

2.8 inches per year

That's how much you might grow this year if you're aged five or six! But everyone's different so keep measuring.

3 feet per day

How much can bamboo
grow in a day?

456 feet
Pyramids of Giza

3 feet
About two of these
books opened wide

Tall, Taller, Tallest!

Mount Everest is the highest mountain on Earth. It is so high that there is very little oxygen for us to breathe up there. Men and women must wear special oxygen masks. Just like you, Mount Everest is still growing bigger every year. If you look up from its base, you would not see its top!

Measure out a foot. What can you fit in that space? What could you fit in a mountain?

29,029 feet
Mount Everest

Surprisingly High

In the shade of woody trees and amongst the shrubs, a froghopper leaves little pools of foamy spit. Have you seen it? Tiny as they are, these little insects have a great skill ...

They can hop 28 inches into the air. That's 400 times their height. If humans could do the same, we would easily go higher than a skyscraper. How high can you hop?

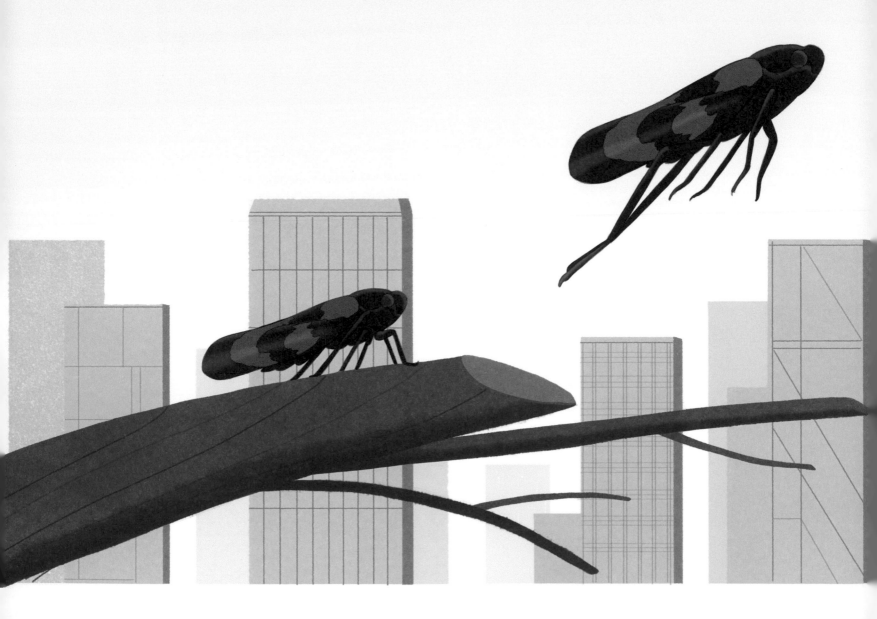

Human vs. a skyscraper

Faster Than a Starfish

Run like the wind and see how fast you can go.

Do you think you are faster than a red deer? It runs a 100-meter dash (which is 328 feet) in just 5 seconds.

Or how about the fastest human? Usain Bolt ran a 100-meter dash in 9.58 seconds.

2 hours
Starfish

You?

Well, I bet you are faster than the fastest starfish. It would take more than 2 hours for the starfish to finish a 100-meter dash.

5 seconds
Red deer

9.58 seconds
Usain Bolt

Sneeze like a Hurricane

Hurricanes rip and rage. They blow and howl a mighty wind. When they grow strong, they can be a deadly danger!

For a wind to turn from a breeze into a hurricane, it must go 75 miles per hour.

SNEEZE
100 mph

But did you know that when sneezing, the particles can fly out of your nose at a speed of 100 miles per hour! You could sneeze with the speed of a hurricane, or a fast car.

Hurricane 75 mph

Deadly hurricane 156 mph

Ferocious but Small

Back in the time when dinosaurs thumped across the land, there were many that were large and tall. The largest was a family of Titanosaurus found in Argentina.

This vegetarian giant was 130 feet long. It's three times the size of Sue, the biggest T. rex ever found.

But not all dinosaurs were so big. One of the smallest is called "Pretty Jaw"—it was smaller than a mountain goat.

3.3 feet long
"Pretty Jaw"

4.3 feet long
Mountain goat

40.4 feet long
Sue, the T. rex

130 feet long
Titanosaurus

Hotter Than Hot

What is the hottest thing you can think of? Are you thinking of the Sun?

The Sun's surface burns and glows at a temperature you can hardly imagine. Yet, there is something hotter than the Sun's surface, and that is a bolt of lightning.

Water boils at 212 degrees Fahrenheit, but your delicious cup of hot chocolate is best sipped at around 136 degrees Fahrenheit.

Now stick your finger under your arm. Your body temperature should be around 98.6 degrees Fahrenheit.

10,340°F   Sun's surface

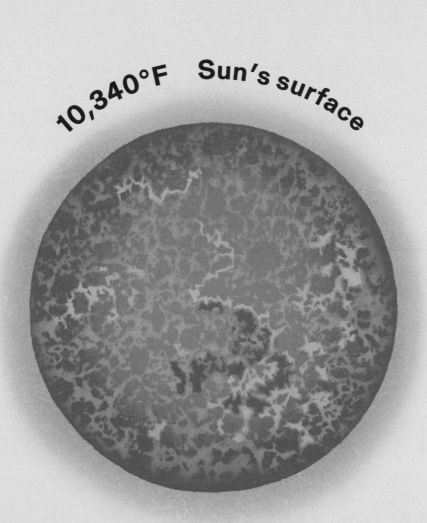

Colder Than Ice

-132°F
The coldest place on Earth, Antarctica

-58°F
Temperature at which
the polar fox can live

Could you walk happily in a land of ice? How cold would you feel without a jacket? How quickly would you come running back to the fire? A polar fox can live without a worry at temperatures below -58 degrees Fahrenheit.

32°F
Water freezes to ice

Walk like a Snowflake

When winter snowflakes come tumbling down from a cloud, the tiny drops of feathery cold seem to glide and dance to the ground.

From 1,000 feet high, it takes them 5 minutes to reach you and me.

If we measure how fast that is, it is like the speed of a slow walk. So go ahead ... walk like a snowflake, dance and glide.

How long does it take you to walk one mile?

2.2 mph
Speed of a snowflake
falling

2.5 mph
Average adult walking speed

So Small, so Heavy

There is a beetle that is 5 inches long. Its name is Goliath.

The Goliath beetle hatches out of an egg, which we call a larva. The Goliath's larva is incredibly large for an insect. It weighs more than a bar of chocolate.

How much did you weigh as a baby? How much do you weigh now?

3.9 OUNCES
Goliath beetle larva

3.5 oz
Chocolate bar

0.09 oz
Etruscan mouse

How much?!

Saliva, or spit, is made every day to keep our mouths watery and healthy.

You may not realize it, but in a single day, you and I will each make 50 fluid ounces of saliva.

A person produces 50 fl oz of spit daily. That amount fits in a big water bottle.

Tiny Travelers

Many animals move across the Earth just to survive. They cross forests, oceans, rivers, and mountains.

But it is not always the biggest and strongest that go the furthest. A little bird called the Arctic tern flies around 24,000 miles per year.

The majestic monarch butterfly flies 3,000 miles per year.

How far do you travel to get to school?

3,000 miles Monarch butterfly migratio

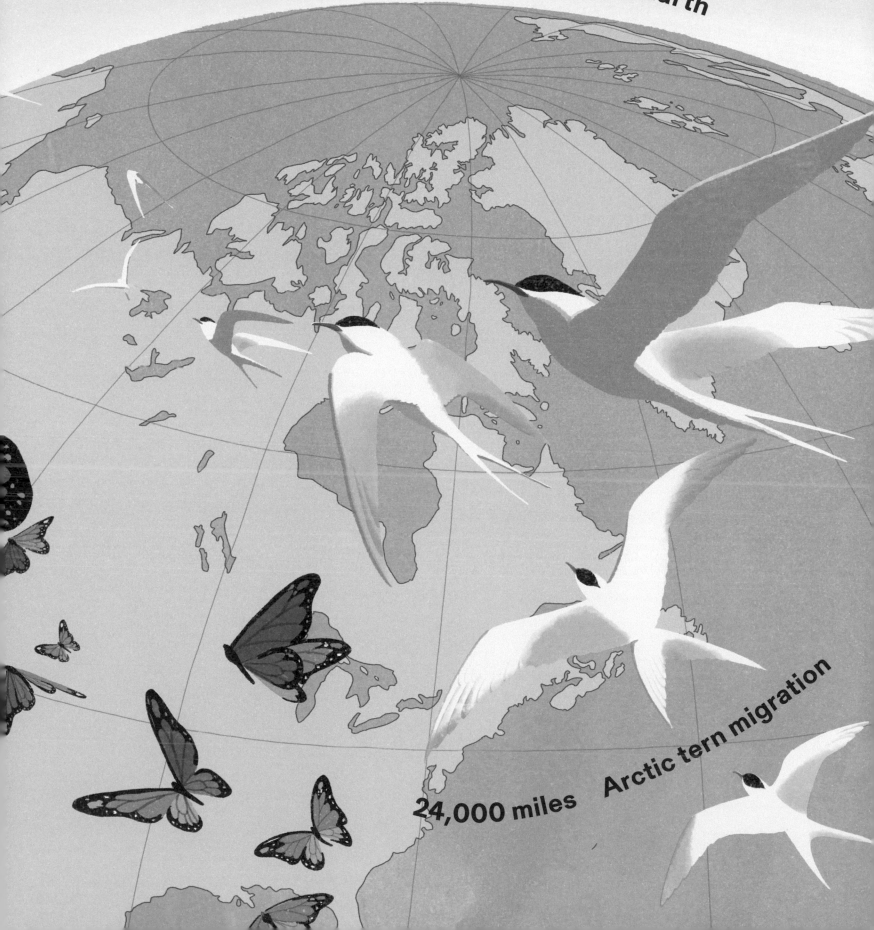

24,901 miles   Distance around the Earth

24,000 miles   Arctic tern migration

Humongous Fungus

What is the biggest thing alive in the world? It is not an elephant or a whale. It is not a giraffe or a tree. Can you guess?

It lives under the ground and grows in a forest in America. The biggest living thing is called Humongous Fungus.

It is a large living chain of fungus that stretches for miles through the soil. Every year, it makes little mushrooms!

If you walked over the length of the Humongous Fungus, would you be able to tell where it began and where it ended?

**3.4 square miles
Size of Humongous Fungus**

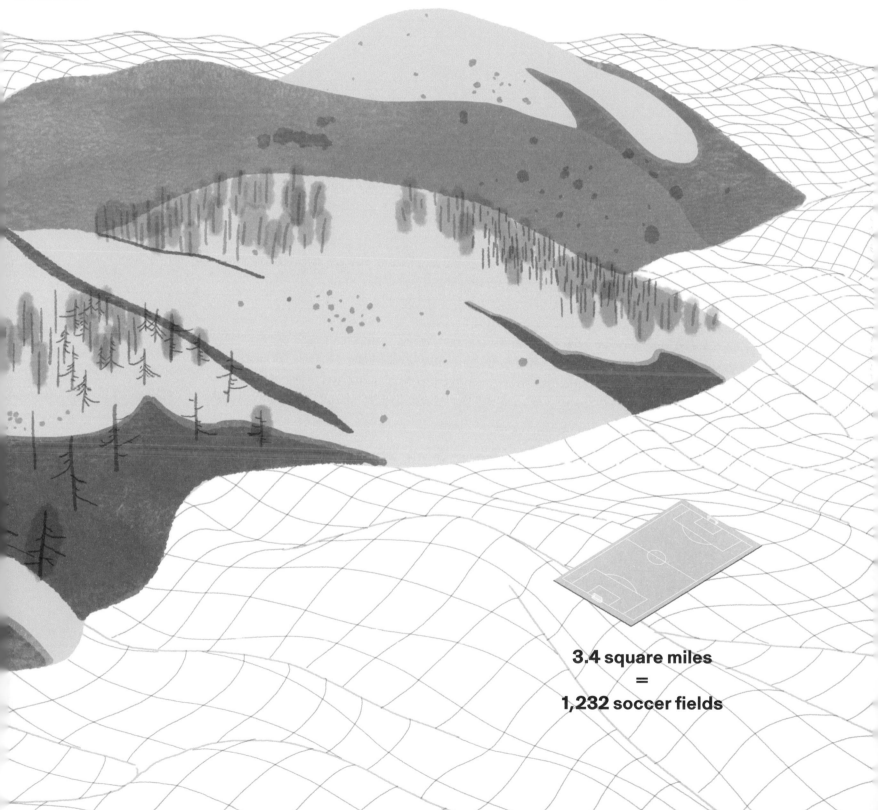

**3.4 square miles
=
1,232 soccer fields**

How can you measure the world?

Try using your arm, or maybe your foot. How many thumbs long is this book? There are many fun ways we can think of for measuring things around us.

It is up to you to try and compare them, and to find surprising things big and small. It is not so hard if you give it a try.

Glossary

Albatross:
A large seabird. Its wings are so big they act like gliders when it flies.

Antarctica:
The southernmost continent on Earth, at the South Pole. It is very cold and covered in ice.

Arctic:
The northernmost region on Earth, surrounding the North Pole. It is a mass of sea that is circled by land.

Arctic tern:
A bird that is born in the Arctic and flies all the way south to the Antarctic for summer.

Bamboo:
A plant that belongs to the grass family. It is the only food a panda will eat.

Colossal squid:
The largest type of squid on Earth. It lives in cold waters and has sharp hooks on the ends of its tentacles.

Dinosaur:
An animal that lived on Earth over 165 million years ago.

The word "dinosaur" means "terrible lizard" in Greek.

Froghopper:
A small insect that leaves a foamy substance on plants. They can be found across Europe and North America.

Giant armadillo:
A mammal that lives in South America. Its body is covered in hundreds of small, hard scales that look like armor.

Goliath beetle:
The heaviest beetle in the world, found in Africa. It has a hard outer shell and six legs.

Honeybee:
A type of bee that makes honey in hives.

Hummingbird:
A small bird with a long bill to suck nectar from flowers. It gets its name from the humming sound its wings make when they flap.

Hurricane:
A violent storm with winds higher than 72 mph.

Monarch butterfly:
A large butterfly from America that travels great distances each year.

Mount Everest:
The tallest mountain on Earth, measured from sea level. It is part of the Himalayan mountain range in Asia.

Otter:
A water mammal with webbed feet and water-repellent fur, which keeps it dry and warm.

Polar fox:
A small white fox that lives in the Arctic. It has thick fur to keep it warm.

Red deer:
A large type of deer with big antlers. You can find red deer in Europe, Asia, and Africa.

Starfish:
Not actually a fish but an invertebrate, which means it has no spine. It likes to eat small sea creatures like snails and clams.

White Mountains:
A mountain range on the East Coast of America.

How Big is Big? How Far is Far? All Around Me

This book was conceived, edited and designed by Gestalten.

Illustrated by Jun Cen

Edited by Robert Klanten and Angela Sangma Francis
Design and layout by Jan Blessing

Research by Kathrin Lilienthal

Typeface: Gerstner Programm
by Christian Mengelt, Karl Gerstner, and Stephan Müller

Printed by Grafisches Centrum Cuno GmbH & Co. KG, Calbe (Saale)
Made in Germany

Published by Little Gestalten, Berlin 2018
ISBN 978-3-89955-812-8

The German edition is available under ISBN 978-3-89955-811-1.
The UK edition is available under ISBN 978-3-89955-780-8.

For more information, please visit little.gestalten.com.

Bibliographic information published by the Deutsche Nationalbibliothek:
The Deutsche Nationalbibliothek lists this publication in the Deutsche Nationalbibliografie;
detailed bibliographic data are available online at dnb.d-nb.de.

This book was printed on paper certified according to the standards of the FSC®.

MIX
Paper from
responsible sources
FSC® C043106